C0-BEJ-750

My First
BIBLE STORIES

PAGE
PUBLICATIONS

CREATION
Genesis 1:3–2:3

In the beginning God created heaven and earth. He made the sun to shine in the daytime and the moon and the stars to shine at night.

God made the sky, the sea, and the land.
He made the birds to fly in the sky and
the fish to swim in the sea.

He made all kinds of animals to roam the land.

Then God created man and woman, Adam and Eve, to care for the earth. God was happy with all he had done and blessed them all.

NOAH'S ARK Genesis 8:19

The Lord said to Noah there will be a great flood. You will need to build an ark big enough for you and your family and two of every animal on earth.

Noah built the ark as God had asked.

When it was finished they gathered two of each animal, large and small, and brought them onto the ark.

It rained for forty days and forty nights.

The whole earth was covered in water but Noah and his family and all the animals were safe in the ark.

When the rain stopped Noah sent a dove to look for
dry land. The dove returned with an olive branch.
Then Noah knew that land was near,
and a beautiful rainbow filled the sky.

DANIEL IN THE LION'S DEN

Daniel 6:22

King Darius had passed a law that no one could pray to anyone except to him or be thrown into the lion's den. Daniel continued to pray to God three times a day. When his enemies saw this they went straight to the king.

The king liked Daniel very much but the law had been broken, so sadly he ordered Daniel thrown into the lion's den. When morning came King Darius went to the den and yelled out "Daniel, did your God save you?" "Yes" said Daniel. "God sent an angel to keep me safe from harm."

THE BIRTH OF JESUS Luke 2:7

Joseph and Mary had been traveling a long way to the city of Bethlehem. When they arrived all the inns were full.

Joseph found a stable that was warm and dry for them to stay. That night Mary gave birth to a baby and his name was Jesus.

THE SHEPHERDS Luke 2

In the fields near Bethlehem there were shepherds watching over their sheep. Suddenly there was a bright light and an angel appeared to them.

"I bring good news" said the angel. "God's special son has been born. You will find him lying in a manger." They hurried at once to go and meet Jesus, the new born king.

FEEDING THE FIVE THOUSAND Matthew 14:19

A large crowd of people had gathered to hear Jesus speak about God. The people had been there all day and some of the disciples suggested to Jesus to send the people away as there was not enough food to feed them all.

They had five loaves of bread and two fish. Jesus gave thanks to God for the food and passed it out to everyone. There was plenty to go around and enough leftover to fill twelve baskets.

JESUS AND THE CHILDREN Luke 18:16

Jesus was teaching about God's love when some children ran up to him. There were grown-ups nearby that said, "Do not bother Jesus. Go away." However, Jesus said "Let the children come to me. God loves the children very much as he loves everyone!"

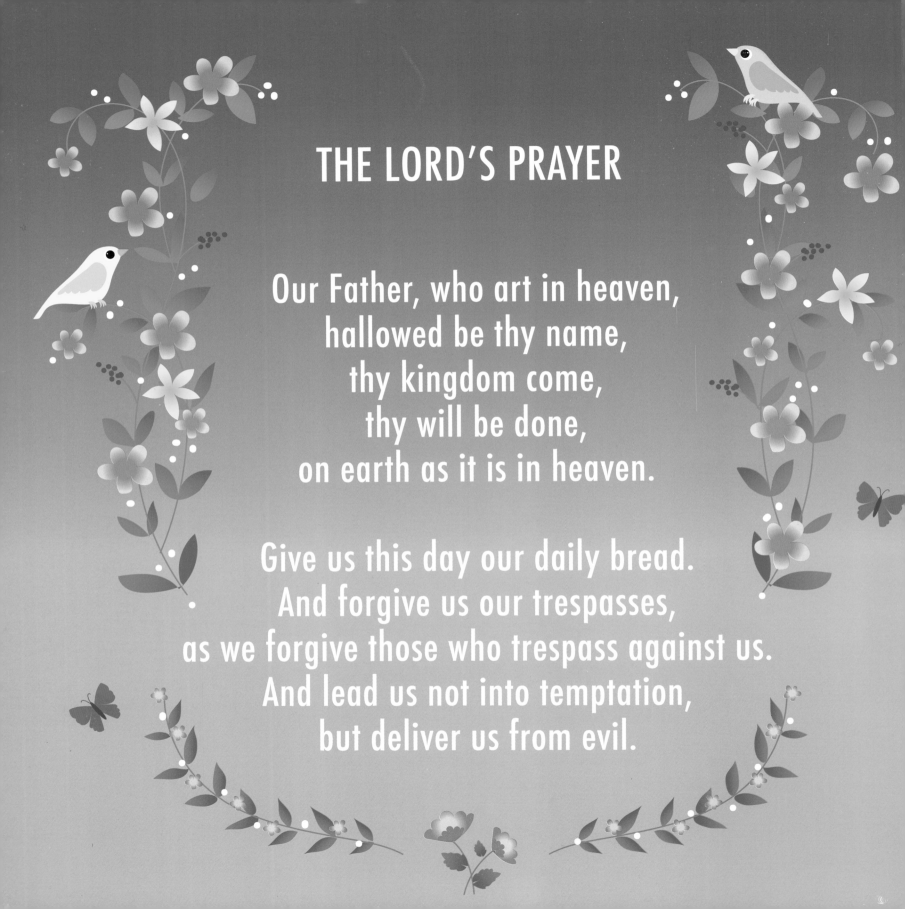

THE LORD'S PRAYER

Our Father, who art in heaven,
hallowed be thy name,
thy kingdom come,
thy will be done,
on earth as it is in heaven.

Give us this day our daily bread.
And forgive us our trespasses,
as we forgive those who trespass against us.
And lead us not into temptation,
but deliver us from evil.